The Prestige S

YELLOWAY

Keith Healey & John Banks

© 2005 Venture Publications Ltd
ISBN 1 898432 45 7

Cover: Most of the chassis bought by Yelloway in the period 1955 to 1979 were AEC Reliances. The Allens were staunch customers of the Southall manufacturer and remained loyal to the Reliance almost as long as it was available, turning to the Leyland Leopard (and then the Tiger) only when it was announced that the Reliance was to be discontinued. The vehicle shown, **WDK 562T**, was one of the last batch of Reliances to enter Yelloway service. It was bodied by Plaxton as a 49-seater and was new in April 1979. *(Geoff Coxon)*

Rear cover: The cover of an early postwar booklet detailing Yelloway Land Cruises. *(Keith Healey Collection/Courtesy Greater Manchester Transport Society)*

Front inside cover: A rather more flamboyant version of the same thing from the prewar period, featuring a small Bedford coach of a type tried by Yelloway in that era. *(Courtesy Dave Haddock Collection)*

Rear inside cover: Yelloway's Weir Street, Rochdale, premises, with a selection of Plaxton-bodied AEC Reliances, in the 1970s. *(Geoff Coxon)*

Title page: **DK 8586** was a Leyland SKP2 Cub, fitted with Bromilow & Edwards 26-seat front-entrance coachwork, new in April 1932. Although it lasted with Yelloway until 1945, it remained unique and no other Cubs were purchased. *(John Banks Collection)*

Opposite page: Yelloway were regular entrants at the Blackpool coach rally and in this 1965 view of AEC Reliance **CDK 856C**, driver Bill Grundy can be seen adding the finishing gloss to the AEC badge on the immaculate Harrington Cavalier coachwork. *(Courtesy Dave Haddock Collection)*

Below: Yelloway were early and enthusiastic users of the new generation of underfloor-engined chassis, placing orders for both Leyland Royal Tigers and AEC Regal IVs, many of which carried the classic Seagull coachwork built by Burlingham. **JDK 320** heads a line of five of 1952's Regal VIs, from the batch of six JDK 320-5. *(Courtesy Dave Haddock Collection)*

Introduction and acknowledgements

Anybody who was involved in the coaching industry in the North-West during the currency of the Yelloway name would have met the Allens of Rochdale, either father Herbert or son Hubert, or both, at least once in his working life. The Allens between them had created and successfully run one of the largest independent express service operations in Britain: not in respect of the size of the fleet - fifty was about the average over the years - but by the range of services and the area covered in their operation. Yelloway coaches could by the 1970s be seen on regular services as far as Glasgow in the North, Paignton in the South-West, Clacton in the South-East, and at nearly every seaside resort on the coast from Ramsgate to Torquay, plus North Devon, North and South Wales and not forgetting Blackpool and the Fylde Coast, Morecambe and Southport.

The story began in 1932 when the Allens changed the name of their company to Yelloway Motor Services Ltd. Joint author Keith Healey had dealings with them both from 1947 through to the late 1970s, either as booking agent or fellow operator. They were the gentlemen of the industry, shrewd but firm with all in their dealings and decisions. They realised that to prosper in a competitive business they had to work together with other operators; this book tells the story of how, and how well, they accomplished that.

In order to follow the pattern of changes from 1946 through to 1980 and the commencement of deregulation, the London, Torbay, Blackpool and Yorkshire groups of services are dealt with separately, showing how progress was made over the years, while excursions and tours receive a section to themselves as do various other aspects of the story not easily incorporated elsewhere. Lastly, there is a brief description of the fleet, closer detail of which is provided in the captions to the photographs.

It was with great sadness and a sense of inadequacy that the other joint author - the undersigned - took on the task of completing this book following the death at the age of 74 of Keith Healey on 29th December 2004.

Keith was a gentleman, ever ready to share his vast knowledge of the coaching industry, particularly as it pertained to the North-West, with other enthusiasts, either personally by helping in many different ways or, in his capacity as author or joint author of a variety of publications, through his writings for the enthusiast press. Keith's works on *Tyne-Tees-Mersey* (written jointly with Philip Battersby), *Associated Motorways*, *Yorkshire Coaching Pools*, and *Hebble* (written jointly with Nicholas Harris), all published by Venture Publications Ltd, have quickly established themselves as authoritative reference books. Keith's ability to look at a photograph and instantly say what service the vehicle was on, what direction it was going in, what timing it was working on what day of the week was little short of miraculous; the undersigned does not have that skill and Keith's absence at the end of a telephone line to quickly and effortlessly solve a maddening query, or at home to welcome a visitor when many such queries and difficulties would be expertly cleared up, means that this book will not be what it might have been had we not lost him and had he had the opportunity of fine-tuning and polishing - an activity that gave him so much pleasurable frustration with his earlier writings.

Yelloway was one of Keith's favourite subjects, however, and the book is offered - warts and all - as a memorial to a great enthusiast and a much-missed friend.

Acknowledgement is made to the book *The Yellow Road*, by Judith and Peter Deegan (1982, Pride Books), to John Dixon for word-processing Keith's original notes, to Ron Maybray and Brian Thackray for vehicle details, to John Gillham for the superb 1974 map, to the Greater Manchester Transport Society for the loan of Yelloway ephemera and photographs, to Mary and Dave Shaw for reading the proofs and, above all, to Dave Haddock, without whom the book could not have been completed; Dave has generously made available the entire contents of his marvellous Yelloway Museum and has vetted the text and captions. It has been a pleasure to use further examples of the fine photography of Geoffrey Atkins and of the late Geoff Coxon.

John Banks
Romiley, Cheshire
April 2005

YELLOWAY

MOTOR SERVICES LTD.

IN ASSOCIATION WITH

ASSOCIATED MOTORWAYS

COMMENCING
SOUTHWARDS
SAT. AUG. 22nd, 1936, to
SAT., SEPT. 26th, 1936.

COMMENCING
NORTHWARDS
SUN. AUG. 23rd, 1936, to
SUN., SEPT. 27th, 1936

BLACK & WHITE, RED & WHITE, MIDLAND "RED," GREYHOUND ROYAL BLUE. UNITED COUNTIES.

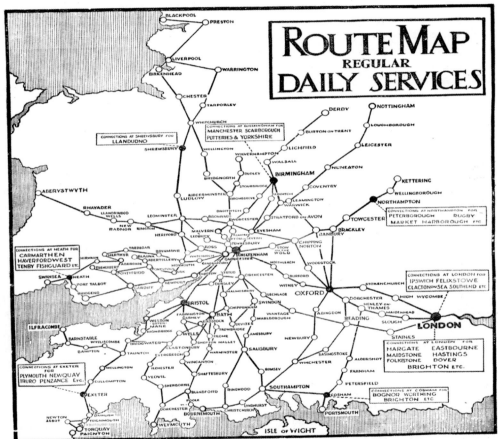

The Yelloway "in association with Associated Motorways" network of regular daily services in 1936. (John Banks Collection)

ROCHDALE
OLDHAM, MANCHESTER, ALTRINCHAM, NEWCASTLE-UNDER-LYME, STAFFORD
— TO —
SOUTH COAST
SALISBURY, SOUTHAMPTON, BOURNEMOUTH, SOUTHSEA, WEYMOUTH, WESTON-SUPER-MARE, TORQUAY, ILFRACOMBE
— AND —
SOUTH WALES
NEWPORT, CARDIFF, SWANSEA, TREHERBERT, MERTHYR.

The beginnings 1932 - 1944

In April 1932 the new directors of Holt Bros. (Rochdale) Ltd changed the name of the company to Yelloway Motor Services Ltd. They had received road service licences from the newly formed Traffic Commissioners for a range of express services, though some were only operated after appeals to the Minister of Transport. London was covered by two routes, one from Blackpool and the other from east Lancashire; they both converged on Manchester and then took the scenic route through Derby, Leicester and Northampton.

The South-West of England, Bristol, Exeter and Torquay had a thrice-weekly service, starting from Rochdale via Manchester, south Cheshire and the Potteries. Blackpool was covered by daily services from Oldham and Rochdale via the Rossendale Valley. Lastly, a limited stop service between Rochdale and Manchester operated every twenty minutes.

There was also a programme of excursions and tours ranging from the normal day or half-day trips to a comprehensive selection of extended tours of from four to nine days' duration throughout Britain and even onto the Continent. It had been an uphill struggle to reach this situation.

Herbert Allen had left the family business of Allen Motors (Bacup) Ltd after the sale of their motor coaches, to join Holt Brothers as Traffic Manager; the company used Yelloway as its fleet name. His son, Hubert, followed him a few years later. The period 1927 to 1929 saw the commencement of a variety of services some of which survived, but others had a short life against the competition that was then springing up every day. Traffic was diminishing and costs were rising. Most of the

Above: The inside cover and first page of a circa 1930 booklet advertising tours operated by Holt Bros. (Rochdale) Ltd. Herbert Allen is listed as Traffic Manager.

>> Opposite page lower: DK 335, a circa 1921 Dennis, photographed in 1926. A very young Hubert Allen stands with his hand on the mudguard of the bus. (Both: Courtesy Dave Haddock Collection)

Above: In the earlier years of the road passenger-carrying industry the expression "dual-purpose" had a different meaning from that which it took on later. Then it meant a vehicle that could be used - usually during the week - for freight or, with a precarious passenger compartment mounted on the lorry platform, as a pleasure conveyance at weekends or on other special occasions. It all looks unpleasantly grimy, not to say dangerous, even by the standards of the day, as Foden steamer *M 2602* sets out on the first ever Holt Brothers passenger trip, from Milnrow Road, Rochdale, to Hollingworth Lake on Saturday, 23rd July 1910. (Courtesy Dave Haddock Collection)

Left: The father: Herbert Allen, MBE, Managing Director of Yelloway from 1931 to 1956.
Right: The son: Hubert Allen, OBE, photographed in 1967. Hubert was MD from his father's death in December 1956 until his retirement in 1985. (Both: Courtesy Dave Haddock Collection)

fleet belonging to Holts was on hire purchase: the inevitable happened, coaches were repossessed and in the end a Receiver was appointed to run the company.

By 1930 the new Road Traffic Act, then going through Parliament, was about to remove the control of licences to operate services from local authorities to the Traffic Commissioners, which were initially based in thirteen Traffic Areas.

Although both the Allens had temporarily lost their jobs at Holts due to staff cuts, they were behind the scenes preparing applications for road service licences; Herbert Allen prepared two applications - one for Holt Brothers, the other in his own name based on his Milnrow home address. Problems could have arisen because the Allens did not own any vehicles at that time, and the second application was withdrawn.

In March 1931 an agreement was reached whereby the Holts resigned from the Board and Herbert Allen and John Barlow were named as directors of the company. The Receiver then returned control of the remaining vehicles to the company after the Allens together with Maurice Edwards and John Barlow had raised the necessary funds to settle with the creditors. The purchase of the Holts' shares was finalised a month later. Maurice Edwards was also made a director and shortly afterwards John Barlow resigned from the Board.

If licences were to be obtained it was necessary to operate the services as per the applications and to show to the Traffic Commissioners that the company was being reconstructed on sound business lines. In general the North Western Traffic Commissioners tried to help the little man to obtain licences and in some cases only granted them if there was coordination of timetables on routes where more than one operator ran. However, on express services the railways sought protection of their services, which the

Above: DK 3742 was a Reo Major with Lewis and Crabtree 20-seat dual-doorway coachwork. The vehicle was new in April 1926, apparently passing into the control of Receivers and then being repurchased in February 1931. Reo chassis were popular with many operators in the mid late 1920s, not least with Holt Brothers, who had at least two dozen.

Below: DK 5482, a 1929 Gilford 1660T, also had Lewis and Crabtree coachwork. A front-entrance 30-seater, it was repossessed when little more than a year old. (Both: Courtesy Dave Haddock Collection)

Traffic Commissioners were obliged to take into consideration when hearing applications.

In the case of the Torquay service many operators applied for licences mainly to operate at weekends only, but were for various reasons refused. The Yelloway route had carried 4,924 passengers in 1931 but the Western Traffic Area chairman refused a backing licence principally on the grounds "that those who wished to stay in Torquay could travel by train of which there was an ample service, or use the established Express Carriage Services". He also considered that during Wakes holidays those who desired to travel to such places as Torquay for the purpose of seeing the country could best do so by means of extended tours. The company appealed against the decision and the Minister overturned it in March 1932 but the condition was added "that no passenger shall be carried in the Western Traffic Area who does not hold a ticket in respect of a journey to or from a point on the route outside the said area". During the period 1st April - 13th September 1931, 830 passengers alighted at Bristol for connecting services elsewhere.

On the London service the Commissioners took the view that there was room for more than one operator from Blackpool and granted licences to W C Standerwick, Scout Motor Services and Wood Brothers as well as to Yelloway. While only Scout had a night service this took a different route from that of Yelloway. There was one other operator, C Smith, owned by Bracewells of Colne, who operated to Blackpool via Darwen and Blackburn from London.

Originally the Yelloway route had continued like the Smith operation taking in such places as Bury, Rawtenstall, Accrington and Blackburn before reaching Preston then Blackpool. The Traffic Commissioners had commented on the Yelloway route but granted a licence from Blackpool and Preston direct to Manchester and a feeder from Rochdale and Oldham to connect at Manchester. The company was determined to win back the east Lancashire section and applied for the Rochdale feeder to be extended. This was granted as far as Haslingden but not Accrington or Blackburn. A further attempt was made in 1932 to extend the route with partial success. Although Accrington and Blackburn were granted there was a condition - no passengers could be carried who were travelling beyond Hockliffe to Dunstable, St Albans and London. This was to protect the Bracewell service, which had given up the Blackpool extension and now operated direct from Colne to London.

There was one other company on the road, Roscoe's, which operated a day and night

<< Opposite page: At "Nancy's" Black Bull Hotel, Oswaldtwistle, 1928 Reo Pullman **DK 4949** has pulled in for a refreshment stop with, behind it, another operator's fine Leyland Lioness. The Reo was another to be repossessed, but was bought back in April 1931.

Above: A number of Tilling-Stevens chassis were acquired in 1929, including **DK 5914**, a Warwicks-bodied 32-seater. Although some of the Tillings were repossessed, this one was not, and survived to be withdrawn by Yelloway in 1945.

Below: **DK 7250**, a Vulcan Prince 32-seater, is seen when brand new outside its coachbuilders, Bromilow & Edwards. This vehicle was withdrawn in 1943. (All: Courtesy Dave Haddock Collection)

service from Preston to London as well as summer weekend services to Glasgow, Torquay and Aberystwyth from Manchester. Because of financial problems, this company ceased trading in 1932. Other coach operators tried to restore the services: Finglands applied to extend their London service to commence from Preston without success; Yelloway applied for a picking up point at Bolton, which was granted then lost on appeal with a restriction being imposed as on the Accrington and Blackburn picking up points. A later application to pick up at Bolton on the night service was granted but the day service restriction remained.

In 1933 there was a general revision of fares from Derby southwards. These included reductions to come into line with other operators on the route such as Yorkshire Services and United Counties. Again in 1937 further reductions took place.

In 1934 a unique system of coordination was brought into being with the introduction of the Associated Motorways network based at Cheltenham. (The full story is told in Prestige Series Number Eighteen *Associated Motorways*.) Yelloway had always offered connecting facilities to the other destinations from their Torquay Service. Gloucester was the changing point for the Red & White services to South Wales, while at Bristol the Greyhound services connected to Bournemouth and Ilfracombe as well as local services to Bath and Weston-super-Mare. Further south connections were made at Taunton with the Lavender Blue services of Thomas Motors to Minehead and at Exeter with various Devon General routes.

The Associated Motorways scheme meant that some of the connections were not always available and on 22nd August 1936 the Yelloway route was diverted to serve Cheltenham and all the connecting services. So began a partnership that lasted into the National Express period. Associated Motorways even went to the trouble of printing a special four-page foolscap-sized leaflet headed *In Association with Yelloway Motor Services* to publicise the connections.

By now the company had become established on the passenger scene and over the years approaches by various operators, including the North Western Road Car Company and Red & White Services, were

made to take over Yelloway, but the Allens were never tempted to sell.

In 1939 the outbreak of the Second World War resulted in the withdrawal of all the services with the exception of the Rochdale-Manchester, which prospered throughout the war years having local fares introduced by the Regional Transport Commissioner for the duration of the War. However, the service and ten vehicles were sold to the Corporations of Manchester, Oldham and Rochdale for £38,500. The price was divided as follows: Manchester £13,743, Oldham £16,651 and Rochdale £8,106. The receipts had increased from £14,269 in 1939 to £27,157 in 1942 with no increase in fares during that period. Two AEC Regents had been hired from London Passenger Transport Board from 1942-1944 to cover the demand.

The war in Europe ceased in May 1945 with the Far East conflict coming to an end a few months later and the company began moves to recommence the facilities offered by them prior to the outbreak of war.

Torbay Services 1945 - 1980

The service from Rochdale to Torquay recommenced after the war in 1946 operating to its prewar timings on Saturdays, Sundays, Wednesdays and Fridays southwards and Sundays, Mondays, Thursdays and Saturdays northwards, with an additional southbound timing on Friday nights.

In April 1948 application was made to operate the service daily during the summer months but by the time it was granted four months later it was too late to introduce it that year and it commenced operation in 1949. Through bookings were made at Cheltenham with the services operated by Associated Motorways.

The Friday night service saw through vehicles being operated across Cheltenham to Bournemouth and Ilfracombe on special timings introduced by Associated Motorways at 2.30am on Saturday mornings ex-Cheltenham available to Yelloway and Ribble only. The vehicles returned from these resorts on normal Saturday morning timings.

In late 1951 applications were made to operate a winter service between Rochdale and

Above: Bromilow & Edwards were also responsible for the 30-seat front-entrance coachwork on **DK 7943**, a 1932 Leyland Tiger TS4, seen here on private hire work. The other vehicles are a mouth-watering lot, with that at the end of the line being a 1932 Yelloway AEC Regal, again bodied by Bromilow & Edwards.

Below: The Leicester Coaching Agency's booking office in a fine portrait taken on 23rd August 1932 that includes not much of two Yelloway coaches. That on the left, 1932 AEC Regal **DK 7874**, is a rare piece of evidence that Yelloway vehicles carried fleet numbers, in this case **32**; **DK 7378**, the Leyland Tiger TS1 on the right of the picture, was bodied by Burlingham and had entered service as DK 7367. *(Both: Courtesy Dave Haddock Collection)*

express motorway & scenic routes

IN COMFORT BY PULLMAN TYPE COACHES

Departure from: Britannia Airways Terminal,
Avon House, Mabledon Place.
(Off Euston Road)

LONDON
DERBYSHIRE
LANCASHIRE

Abbreviated Time Table

NORTHWARDS

SERVICE Comm. operation·	C 13 May	B (S) 13 May	X 21 Mar.	M 21 Mar.	A 22 Mar.	N 23 Mar.
LONDON dep.	0830	1000	1000	1000	1730	2345
DERBY arr.			1410	1410		0404
STOCKPORT arr.			1609	1609		0559
MANCH'R arr.	1330		1630	1630	2230	0619
BOLTON arr.				1658		0647
PRESTON arr.		1550		1745		0734
BLACKPOOL arr.		1640		1835		0824
OLDHAM arr.	1354	—	1659	—	2254	0644
ROCHDALE arr.	1416	—	1724	—	2316	0706

SOUTHWARDS

SERVICE Comm. operation—	A 22 Mar.	M 20 Mar.	X 20 Mar.	B (S) 13 May	C 13 May	N 22 Mar
BLACKPOOL dep.	—	0800	—	1000	—	2130
PRESTON dep.	—	0850	—	1050	—	2220
BOLTON dep.	—	0937	—			2307
ROCHDALE dep.	0700		0920		1600	2245
OLDHAM dep.	0725		0945		1625	2310
MANCH'R dep.	0800	1015	1015		1700	2345
STOCKPORT dep.		1035	1035			0005
DERBY dep.		1300	1300			0200
LONDON arr.	1300	1620	1620	1640	2200	0623

FOR FULL DETAILS SEE TIME AND FARE TABLE

Map labels: BLACKPOOL, ST. ANNES, PRESTON, BLACKBURN, ACCRINGTON, HASLINGDEN, RAWTENSTALL, BACUP, ROCHDALE, SHAW, OLDHAM, MANCHESTER, STOCKPORT, MACCLESFIELD, BOLTON, M.6. MOTORWAY, LEEK, ASHBOURNE, DERBY, ROUTES M, N & X, ROUTES A, B, C, M.1. MOTORWAY, DUNSTABLE, ST. ALBANS, ROUTES A. B. C, ROUTES M, N & X, GOLDERS GREEN, LONDON

METROPOLITAN CHARTING AGENTS
George Ewer & Co. Ltd.
53-55 Stamford Hill,
London, N. 16.
Phone: STA 1833 or 01-800 1833

5 JOURNEYS DAILY IN EACH DIRECTION **6** ON SATURDAY

Operators: **YELLOWAY MOTOR SERVICES LTD.**
Weir Street, Rochdale. Tel: 47561-2-3-4   and Bloomfield Road, Blackpool. Tel: 45353/4

Above: By July 1967, the date of this advertisement for Yelloway express routes, the attractions - as they were then perceived (Ribble even ran excursions along the new M6) - of travel on motorways were being mentioned. (John Banks Collection)

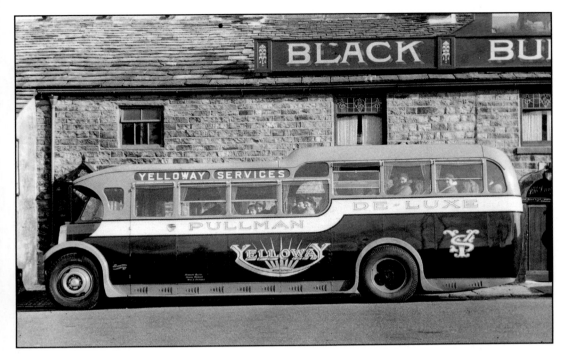

Above: The Black Bull again, with the magnificent **DK 7984**, another 1932 Leyland Tiger TS4, with Bromilow & Edwards observation coach bodywork. Sitting rather uneasily with the prominent fleetname, the livery was an otherwise attractive two-tone blue and cream.

Below: Inside the garage at Weir Street, Rochdale, Jim McDonald and Bert Lewis (who was to lose his life during the Second World War) pose in front of another of the 1931 Burlingham-bodied Leyland Tiger TS1s, **DK 7380**. The vehicle was withdrawn in June 1944. (Both: Courtesy Dave Haddock Collection)

Bristol together with extra night services, Saturday south, Friday and Saturday north, during the summer period. The winter application was changed to terminate at Cheltenham but later withdrawn.

In their evidence Yelloway stated that they had carried 68,000 passengers in 1951 compared with 13,157 in 1947 on the Devonian service. The application was not to carry more passengers but to spread the loads more evenly over the weekends where at the moment the bulk of the traffic northwards was on Saturday mornings. If the Saturday night services had operated many passengers would have taken advantage of another day to their holiday and vehicles would be better utilised instead of travelling empty on Friday and Sunday.

The night service came into operation in 1952 with additional timings again to and from Cheltenham including for the first time connections to Cornwall by Associated Motorways. Ribble also applied for additional timings. A new application was made for a service to Cheltenham, which commenced at Easter 1954.

An Oldham coach operator, Blue Bird Motor Services, had purchased an hotel in Newquay and applied for a service to the resort. Yelloway opposed the application on the grounds that the new connecting facilities to Cornwall the previous year were more than adequate to meet the demand. This was agreed by the Traffic Commissioners and upheld on appeal by the Minister who at the same time stated that a change of vehicle en route could not be classed as an inconvenience to the traveller.

In 1956 an additional pickup point was introduced at Lower Mosley Street bus station, Manchester. This was a help to passengers who travelled from east Lancashire and south Cheshire into Lower Mosley Street who would then have had to make their way to East Street, which was Yelloway's pick-up point.

By now Yelloway was steadily increasing its share of the Associated Motorways traffic on connecting services. Taking the four years 1960-3 inclusive they provided £186,549 worth of business on services from Cheltenham compared with £119,880 by Ribble whilst Royal Blue and the Yorkshire Pool provided a total of £125,270 between them.

The company had always requested names and addresses of passengers to be written on their tickets, mainly to cover any error made, but also as an indication of where their passengers originated. This information was put to good use in 1964 when a new Torquay route was introduced, which ran via Ashton-under-Lyne, Stockport, Macclesfield and Leek to Newcastle under Lyme, where it joined the main route. It enabled passengers to join en route, where previously they had had to go to Manchester, Altrincham or Knutsford to join the coach.

It was decided to introduce joint services with Associated Motorways to replace the Friday night connecting facilities via Cheltenham. 1967 saw Ilfracombe, Weymouth, Bournemouth and Portsmouth dealt with and a year later a new route to Monmouth, Cardiff and Barry Island was introduced.

Also in 1967 Ribble and Yelloway were in discussion about improving the services from east Lancashire to the South-West, as passengers had to travel to Preston to join Ribble or to Manchester for Yelloway services.

A joint service was introduced between Colne and Paignton departing Friday nights and Saturday days southwards calling at Nelson, Burnley, Blackburn, Darwen and Bolton. Through bookings were available via Cheltenham and also on Ribble's X43 service from Skipton to Colne.

At the same time Lancashire United Transport was watching this development with interest and decided to make an application for a service from Swinton to Cheltenham at summer weekends. The Ribble/Yelloway Colne service had some extra picking-up points applied for to cover this application. In the end a joint service was introduced by Lancashire United and Yelloway from Rochdale to Paignton via Swinton.

In order to speed up some of the services, pickups at Wolverhampton, Kidderminster and Tewkesbury were withdrawn from certain timings to the South West.

In 1973 the X65 Colne to Cheltenham service commenced winter operation on Friday to Monday inclusive. The following year saw the introduction of National Travel route numbers to the joint services with Associated Motorways that had been transferred to

Above: We owe to this pair of those informal snapshots, doubtless taken on a simple Kodak Box Brownie, or possibly Vestpocket, camera, that were taken of people, with little thought given to the vehicle, some fine detail of an albeit incompletely illustrated **DK 7381**, yet another of the Burlingham-bodied 1931 Tiger TS1s

Below: AEC Regal **DK 7792**, a 1932 Bromilow & Edwards-bodied 32-seater, is seen in the summer of that year on a Scottish tour. The driver (in the white coat) was Tom Lett. (All: Courtesy Dave Haddock Collection)

National Travel (North West). Although never used they are listed for interest: 925 Colne to Paignton; 960 Rochdale to Ilfracombe; 961 Rochdale to Barry Island; 970 Rochdale to Portsmouth; 971 Rochdale to Weymouth and 972 Rochdale to Bournemouth.

Passengers who wished to travel from the Potteries had to wait until the vehicles had arrived from Rochdale in the mid-morning and in 1975 application was made for a Saturday only service from May to September departing Hanley at 9.05am and connecting with the 11.30am departures from Cheltenham. This meant passengers could reach their destination three hours earlier and Cornwall could be reached during the day thus avoiding night travel. Later the service started at Rochdale.

By now discussions were taking place between National Travel and Yelloway on the coordination of routes, resulting in what was to be known as the 1976 Agreement, which, as far as services to the South-West were concerned, recognised that Yelloway was the principal operator from Greater Manchester, east Lancashire, Cheshire and the Potteries. National gave up its interest in the joint ex-Ribble and Lancashire United services and in the former Associated Motorways services. There had also been on the Ribble and Lancashire United excursions licence from Bolton period returns to Torquay and Bournemouth during Bolton holidays. These destinations had originated with Arthur Christy, an operator purchased by Ribble in 1935. These two excursions were transferred onto a new licence to be held jointly by Yelloway and Lancashire United and operated during Bolton holiday fortnight only.

The Yelloway operating area was also laid down in the Agreement, which taken eastwards made Portsmouth the furthest point reached via Cheltenham; such resorts as Brighton were to be offered via London. This also meant that National Travel agents were able to book more freely on Yelloway services as they were now shown in the National timetable.

Blackpool and the Fylde Coast 1945 - 1980

The Blackpool service recommenced in late 1945 and Yelloway was not the only operator on it. Apart from the period excursions run for

Wakes weeks by local coach companies, Ribble had the X89 from Rochdale. There was also the joint service X9 from Oldham via Manchester and Blackpool operated by North Western, Ribble and Lancashire United plus other services by Ribble as well as W C Standerwick from the Rossendale Area.

In 1954 Hubert Allen and Horace Bottomley, Ribble's General Manager, arranged a meeting to discuss coordination of the Blackpool services to avoid competition as well as reducing mileage. After consultation with George Brook, General Manager of the North Western Road Car Company, an Oldham - Blackpool scheme was presented to the Traffic Commissioners. Two licences were jointly applied for by five operators: Yelloway, Ribble, W C Standerwick, North Western and Lancashire United. The first licence was for service X79 operating daily throughout the year with an additional timing in the summer via Edenfield, which was numbered X89. They both followed the original Yelloway route even terminating at the Yelloway coach station in Bloomfield Road, Blackpool; the second was for the old X9 service but with an additional setting-down point at Bloomfield Road before terminating at the Coliseum. Return tickets were interavailable on each service between common points. There were certain licences to be surrendered including Ribble's Rochdale - Blackpool and Todmorden - Blackpool services as well as Standerwick's Bacup - Blackpool route. Two positioning timings on the Burnley - Rochdale service were also withdrawn; these had been operated so that the Rochdale - Blackpool car did not have to stay overnight in Rochdale. Additional timings to serve the RAF Camp at Weeton, to be operated as required by the camp authorities, were transferred from the surrendered Yelloway licences.

During the Rossendale Valley annual holidays Ribble had operated early timings to cater for holidaymakers as had Yelloway from Rochdale during that town's holidays. These extra facilities were incorporated into the licences but not shown in the general timetable, being advertised only in the areas concerned. In the agreement drawn up for revenue and mileage allocation Yelloway came out with 68.171% and the Pool services commenced 1st April 1955.

Above: The standards of comfort in a 1930s luxury coach were high. This was **ADK 161**, a 1935 Burlingham-bodied Leyland Tiger TS7.

Below: The Bedford WTB 25-seater appeared in the fleet in 1936. **ADK 873** had coachwork by Duple and was one of a batch of four, all of which were withdrawn in 1938. (Both: Courtesy Dave Haddock Collection)

In May 1955 an approach was made to both North Western and Yelloway by Thomas H Parker, trading as Blue Bird Motor Services, of Hollinwood, Oldham, for the sale of his business including seven vehicles, a garage suitable for ten vehicles, plus Hyde - Cleveleys and Oldham - Loggerheads Sanatorium services together with an excursions and tours licence, all for £30,000. Unfortunately, neither company would consider that figure but were prepared to purchase the business at a more reasonable price. A further approach was made by the Parkers (father and son) in October, when it was decided that North Western and Yelloway would purchase only the goodwill of the licences operated. George Brook, acting on behalf of North Western, worked the goodwill out on a rather complicated BET formula as £8,000. Hubert Allen considered it to be more like £12,000 but went along with the lower figure. However, all was not well between the two companies. They both agreed that the Loggerheads service should go to North Western and the Cleveleys service should go into the Oldham - Blackpool Pool, although North Western considered it should have some entitlement to revenue for the picking-up points on the Cheshire side of Oldham. The biggest bone of contention, however, was the excursion licences. Both companies operated excursions from Oldham and each considered that they were entitled to them. In the end Hubert Allen said that he was prepared to enter into competition for this part of the business. The Parkers were approached separately by each company offering the agreed £8,000 and they went away to consider the offer. Perhaps the Parkers thought they had a better chance with Yelloway than North Western and offered the business for £10,000, to which Hubert Allen agreed, thus obtaining the excursion licences.

This left a service operated by North Western between Glossop and Blackpool that had originally commenced from Stalybridge when it was purchased from H Kinder in 1935. This service served all the points that Blue Bird had and was offered to the Blackpool Pool and was later purchased for £2,245. The ex-Blue Bird service was placed in the Pool from 26th March 1956 and numbered X69; the Glossop service came a year later at Easter and was numbered X49.

It was necessary to make further agreements between the joint operators for allocation of mileage and revenue etc. This was signed on 31st December 1957 but backdated to 1st April 1956. As seen in the original agreement, Yelloway had a high revenue allocation but this was to change and to their advantage. Their entitlement was reduced to 50% but they received a payment of £881/5s/0d from the other companies to cover the loss on mileage. They also received a further payment of £3,500 for the Blue Bird Hyde to Cleveleys service from the Pool. The Pool was now advertised as the Fylde Coast Services, a name it retained for many years.

To keep account of revenue, universal vouchers headed "Oldham - Blackpool Services" were issued to agents; the vouchers included the names of all five operators. In order to further publicise the service and increase passenger loadings, special leaflets were printed by Ribble on the Pool's behalf showing connecting facilities at Preston to Southport, Morecambe, the Lake District and Scotland for Oldham and Rochdale as well as from Bury to Morecambe.

In 1959 the originating point at Oldham was renamed from Holts of Oldham, at No. 3 The Mumps, to the Yelloway coach station, thus severing the Holts connection with the Yelloway services.

In 1962 two journeys on the X79 were extended to and from Bispham, Cleveleys and Fleetwood and were operated from Whitsuntide until the end of the illuminations. The extra timings to Weeton RAF Camp were withdrawn at the same time as they were no longer required by the camp.

In 1969 the X49 Glossop - Cleveleys service was extended through to Fleetwood.

The previous year Yelloway had purchased the businesses of North Manchester Motor Services Ltd and William Makinson (Manchester) Ltd, which had been under joint ownership. They were operated as subsidiaries but in 1969 Robert Brook, then General Manager of North Western, found out that North Manchester was still operating its Middleton to Blackpool service. He considered that to be in breach of Clause 26 of the Pool Agreement, whereby the purchase of a company by one of the partners that had been

The Blackpool coachbuilder Burlingham gained orders for many of the Allens' larger coaches in the second half of the thirties. This Leyland Tiger TS7, new in March 1937, was **BDK 990**, a 32-seat rear-entrance coach that survived in this form until May 1951, when it was rebodied by Trans United, lasting thus until 1954. (Both: Courtesy Dave Haddock Collection)

operating in competition with the Pool should be offered to the Pool. After correspondence with Yelloway a meeting was arranged at Preston, where agreement was reached for the Pool to take over not only the North Manchester service but also the revenue from any day or period excursions operated to Blackpool by North Manchester and William Makinson. The sum of £1,692 was to be paid by the Pool to Yelloway for the Blackpool express licence. The service commenced at Easter 1970 and was numbered X19 but this was changed the following year to X29 to avoid clashing with the North Western/Yorkshire Traction X19 Manchester to Barnsley operation. A new operating agreement was signed on 2nd July 1970 but there was no change in mileage or revenue allocation.

In 1971 the Fylde Coast holiday traffic required duplication. This was arranged by Yelloway on the X29, X79 and X89 services and the X9 and X49 were the responsibility of North Western. Unfortunately, Yelloway duplication figures are not available, but North Western provided 27 duplicates for Oldham holidays in that year on the early morning departure whilst the September holidays needed a further 23.

1972 brought further revisions with the X29 now commencing from Hollinwood and the X9 cut back to commence from Middleton instead of Oldham and in 1973 the Blackpool terminal was moved to Talbot Road bus station.

In 1973/4 National Travel (North West) renumbered all the routes into the national 800/900 scheme. This included the Fylde Coast Pool, which were allocated numbers 900 - 994 inclusive; these were never used and the X route numbers continued to be employed.

The 1976 agreement drawn up between National Travel (NBC) Ltd and Yelloway, as far as the Fylde Coast Pool was concerned, caused all the routes to be transferred to Yelloway, with National Travel surrendering all their joint licences.

The timetable dated 7th April 1977, although printed by Ribble, showed Yelloway as the sole operator and in the same year an application was made to transfer one of the Ribble Bolton to Blackpool licences to Yelloway with all fare stages deleted except between the terminal points. This became X99.

Also in 1977 the X9 ceased to Manchester (Chorlton Street coach station), henceforth by-passing the city completely.

October 1980 brought about the deregulation of express services and the way Yelloway coped with the problem is shown in the section detailing the period 1981 - 1986.

Yelloway in Yorkshire 1945 - 1980

The company always had a foot in Yorkshire going back to the Holt Brothers era. This included feeder services from Todmorden and Hebden Bridge to Rochdale during the former towns' annual holidays and through bookings to London and Torquay. This was later extended when the purchase of Creams (Lancashire) Ltd in 1947 brought in a service to Llandudno picking up in Todmorden and Hebden Bridge, to which were later added Elland and Halifax.

Yelloway also had working arrangements with Hanson's of Huddersfield whereby passengers could travel from Huddersfield to Oldham on Hanson's local service to connect with the Torquay service; a similar arrangement was made with Hebble of Halifax from that town to Rochdale for onward connections. These through-booking arrangements could be traced back to the early 1930s; they recommenced after the war when the Devonian service was restarted.

Numbers of passengers carried increased each year with Hanson's and Hebble operating through vehicles across Oldham and Rochdale to Torquay. Through coaches were also to cross Cheltenham on hire to Associated Motorways from that town to Bournemouth and Southsea.

The local independent operators in the West Riding considered that the traffic should be theirs and Wallace Arnold, J W Kitchen, O & C Holdsworth and Hanson's applied separately for licences from their operating areas to Torquay or Paignton. Objections were lodged against these services by the Yorkshire Services Pool, Associated Motorways, Hebble and Yelloway but before the applications could be heard they were withdrawn, being replaced by a joint application by the four operators, which also attracted objections. Yelloway were well aware that if this was granted it would lose a substantial part of its traffic from Huddersfield.

Above: When **BDK 990** was rebodied to front-entrance specification by Trans United, it seems that some parts from the original Burlingham body were used, or at least closely copied, particularly in the area of the cab front and the destination screens. *(John Banks Collection)*

Below: Four more Duple-bodied 25-seat Bedford WTBs came in 1937 and were rather longer-lived than the 1936 batch, lasting into the second half of the 1940s. Tom Lett was again in charge, in a view of **CDK 8** at Great Glen. *(Courtesy Dave Haddock Collection)*

The response was to apply for a feeder service from Huddersfield to Manchester (East Street) to connect with the Torquay route.

Yorkshire Services also applied to increase the facilities they offered via Birmingham. When the applications came up before the Yorkshire Traffic Commissioners they were all refused with the Minister upholding that decision on appeal. Certain observations were made by the Minister: he did not agree with the Yorkshire Chairman that linking of licences together with through running should be banned as this would be against public interest, but suggested that if this was the intention of the operators it should be declared on their application and shown on the licence. He did rule that objectors could only lodge objections against, and be heard in connection with, services that they were licensed to operate and not on any linked arrangements that they had arranged with other operators.

Two years later further applications were lodged with the Traffic Commissioners by Wallace Arnold, J W Kitchen and Hanson for separate licences to Torquay from their respective areas, i.e. Leeds, Bradford and Huddersfield, restricted to July and August only. To combat this Yorkshire Services applied for a direct Torquay service, with Yelloway and Hebble jointly applying for a weekend service from Bradford via Halifax and Huddersfield to Torquay. Objections were lodged by the railways and cross objections by the applicants.

There were two forms of objections to applications depending upon circumstances: the first was that with no chance of succeeding but which was gone through with on the principle of protecting the objector's interests and in the hope of limiting the licence granted. The second was the fight to the finish when Counsel for both sides asked and gave no quarter; evidence was not given under oath and matters were sometimes conducted over-enthusiastically. Such was the case at this hearing.

As far as Wallace Arnold and J W Kitchen were concerned, they were applying for a facility that was not available: a through service to Torquay. In the case of Hanson it was not quite as simple. Their evidence of need was based on names and addresses of intending passengers who wished to travel by Yelloway

and had indeed done so on earlier occasions who had enquired at Hanson's Huddersfield booking office. Hanson had refused to book them, explaining they were applying for a service of their own direct from Huddersfield and would put their name on the waiting list. Hanson also refused to hire vehicles to Yelloway as in previous years on the pretext they were fully committed for the forthcoming season. This brought about the argument that Hanson was bound by common law as an agent for Yelloway to pass on any bookings that passengers wished to make. This was of course not being done and appropriate corroboratory evidence had been obtained by Yelloway.

On the first day of the hearing, Wallace Arnold questioned the right of the objectors to be heard as none of them was licensed to operate to Torquay. The Chairman upheld this and granted representation only to the objectors which meant they had no recourse to appeal. The hearing was adjourned and after considering the matter the Chairman granted full rights to the objectors and the hearing continued a few days later.

The hearing was spread over twelve days from May to September 1956. Yelloway received a rough ride during the hearing, being accused of being its own Licensing Authority in introducing through vehicles to Torquay, flouting the law and operating irregularly. The company had duplicated other people's stage carriage services by superimposing express services granted by themselves.

Hanson, although acknowledging that they did have a linking arrangement at Oldham, also claimed that many of the duplicates, although carrying Hanson "On Hire" labels, were operated without their knowledge. Yelloway in their evidence stated that in 1955 they carried 6,403 passengers from Bradford, Halifax and Huddersfield to Torquay.

The Traffic Commissioners reserved their decision and in December granted to Wallace Arnold, J W Kitchen and Hanson a restricted licence for the annual holiday period of Leeds, Bradford and Huddersfield with one town to each operator. Hanson was granted a four-vehicle allocation, which was not very great considering that Yelloway had operated 14 vehicles the previous year on that date. All the other applications were refused.

*Above: A bold move in 1938 was to place an order for three Leyland Titan TD5 double-deckers, with 56-seat rear-entrance, open-platform bodies, two by Leyland and one by Burlingham. The Leyland-bodied pair, DDK 256/7, are represented by **DDK 256** when brand new.*

Below: The luxurious interiors and fine attention to detail, as well as the door enclosing the lower saloon from the platform, are shown in these views. In the rear view, the deep gloss paintwork reflects the adjacent wall's brickwork as if in a mirror. (All: John Banks Collection)

Appeals were lodged against the grants but the Minister upheld the decision and Yelloway continued the through-running in conjunction with Hebble from Bradford and Halifax to the South-West.

In 1964 Malcolm Barr of Wallace Arnold approached Hubert Allen to discuss the possibility of a scheme to operate services to the South-West. It was decided to consult Norman Dean, General Manager of Yorkshire Traction, for the views of the Yorkshire Service operators. When they all met they found Associated Motorways had put forward the idea of their Cheltenham to Derby service being extended to Sheffield. After discussions a joint application was lodged by Wallace Arnold, J W Kitchen, Yorkshire Services, Associated Motorways, Hebble and Yelloway. Whether or not Hanson was consulted and decided not to join is not recorded.

The consortium was known as the Yorkshire - Torbay Pool Partners and licences were applied for in that name. On the first day of the hearing the applications fell apart with the Counsel for the objectors submitting that the applicants did not constitute a legal partnership and this caused the application to be withdrawn.

In January 1966 another attempt was made with all the operators submitting separate applications for the four services with the consideration that they were to be jointly operated with each other. When the hearing resumed the objectors again raised various points of law.

Again the hearing was relisted, this time for six days commencing Wednesday 9th September 1966, some 17 months after the original applications had been made. This caused one leading trade paper to comment: "They seemed to have stirred up nearly as much commotion as the landings of the invasion forces of William of Orange at Torbay on November 5th 1688".

Licences were granted although only for the summer season and there was a duplication restriction. The Yorkshire Traffic Commissioner seemed to bend over towards the railways and agree to restrictions where none was really needed whereas other Chairmen were quite happy to let the traffic cater for itself. After all, the railways' biggest competitor was the motor-car as it was also of the express coach operators. Restrictions were placed on some picking-up points to protect the weekend holiday services of Sheffield United Tours and G C Littlewood and finally the extra duplication granted on the Yorkshire Services route to Birmingham for onward running to Cheltenham was rescinded.

With Yelloway having the largest revenue and mileage stake in the Pool (28.36%), the facility in conjunction with Hebble was withdrawn, both companies henceforth providing vehicles direct from Yorkshire.

The first journey on the South West Clipper, as the service was advertised, was on 1st May 1967, when 29 passengers were carried on a Yorkshire Traction vehicle.

Traffic from Yorkshire to South Wales was going to be dealt with differently whereby passengers travelled on the Yorkshire Services Pool route to Birmingham and changed to Associated Motorways direct services to South Wales via the M5 and M50 motorways. However, because of the withdrawal of the extra vehicles licensed to Birmingham, it was anticipated that problems would arise and connections were still shown via Cheltenham on the Clipper leaflets.

Winter operation from Yorkshire to Cheltenham commenced on 1st October 1969 and two years later a direct service between Bournemouth and Bradford, marketed as the Bournemouth Clipper, was introduced.

In 1972 Yelloway had difficulty in meeting their commitments on the South West Clipper, having to pay £3,005.70 in connection with vehicles hired from other members to cover Yelloway's share of the mileage.

London and Clacton on Sea Services 1945 - 1980

The routes between Blackpool and Blackburn, London and Clacton on Sea, were closely intertwined. From 1946 the London services resumed as before the outbreak of war in 1939. The principal route commenced at Blackpool and ran via Preston, Chorley and Bolton, still with the restriction on passengers being picked up or set down at Bolton for points to and from Dunstable, St Albans, Golders Green and London on the day service.

*Above: The last of the three Leyland Titan TD5s, **DDK 441**, was the one bodied by Burlingham. (Senior Transport Archive)*

*Below: A rare in-service view of one of the double-deckers. Leyland-bodied **DDK 256** was heading into Manchester and about to overtake a municipal double-decker. The three Titans were withdrawn in June 1944 and passed one each to Oldham, Rochdale and Manchester Corporations. (John Banks Collection)*

The second route started at Blackburn and ran via Accrington, Haslingden, Rossendale Valley, Rochdale and Oldham to Manchester where it joined the route from Blackpool. A condition of the licences and others issued later was that only enough vehicles to carry passengers south of Manchester need be operated. In many cases the route from Blackburn was used as a feeder, passengers changing at Manchester to the vehicle from Blackpool when traffic was light. The prewar restriction relating to south of Hockliffe from Blackburn and Accrington still applied.

Two events occurred in London in the early 1950s: the Festival of Britain and the Coronation of Queen Elizabeth II. The 1951 Festival ran from May to September and an additional vehicle allowance was granted to carry passengers attending it to London only during the Festival period.

1953 again brought about an extra vehicle allowance. Twenty-four vehicles were granted per day in each direction during May, June and July for the Coronation and its attendant festivities. In both cases there was a restriction that the extra vehicles should not be used to convey passengers between Loughborough and points to London.

In 1956 arrangements were made with Premier Travel of Cambridge to offer through bookings via Leicester to Cambridge, Colchester and Clacton on Sea on Premier's service 5 from Birmingham. The connection operated on Saturdays only from mid June until mid September. The same year saw the lifting of the restriction on the Bolton day service so that it could serve London.

Although Loughborough, Leicester and Northampton were many miles from Rochdale, Yelloway was the principal daily operator from those towns to Blackpool. Agreement was reached with the operators of services from the above-mentioned towns to London: as long as Yelloway did not seek to extend the duplication condition to include London they would not object to extra facilities to Blackpool during the annual holiday periods of those towns. The Traffic Commissioners required the company to keep records of passengers carried on the Easyway Holiday scheme whereby hotel accommodation and coach travel could be booked at an inclusive charge.

In 1961 new through services to Blackpool and Blackburn from Clacton on Sea were introduced to replace the connection at Leicester. Numbered 74 and 75 in the Premier Travel series, they operated on Friday nights and Saturday days in each direction during the summer months.

In 1964 two further services were introduced on the Clacton route again carrying Premier Travel numbers, this time 77 and 78. By changing at Haverhill, through bookings were available to Felixstowe on the Premier Travel service numbered 66. At the same time application was made to extend the weekend services to Clacton throughout the winter.

Over the years anybody wishing to travel from Derby to London had to wait until either Yelloway or Yorkshire services arrived from the north or make their way to Nottingham and travel thence by United Counties services. Attempts had been made to start a service from Alfreton without success; however, after a series of Traffic Court hearings the Derbyshire Express was introduced on 5th April 1965 commencing at Alfreton and running through Heanor to Derby, where connection was made at Derby Midland railway station with the London train, then via Kegworth, Loughborough and Leicester. It was operated jointly by Trent, Midland General, United Counties and Yelloway. This was the first time Trent or Midland General had had a London licence and was the only occasion when a Yelloway vehicle operated into Victoria coach station in London with tickets being inter-available with the Yelloway route.

One year later two further new services were introduced jointly with Grey Green of London operating from Blackpool via Haslingden to Ramsgate on Friday nights southwards and Saturday days northwards during the summer months. These replaced the through bookings made with Orange Luxury Coaches from King's Cross coach station in London to Margate and Ramsgate.

A Saturdays-only service between Bedford and Blackpool was introduced on the Clacton licence. At the same time additional services were licensed jointly by Yelloway, Premier Travel, Midland Red and Ribble between Bedford - Southport and Bedford - Morecambe. Yelloway and Premier would between them

*These interior views are of **DDK 441**, the Burlingham-bodied Leyland Titan TD5, which also had the lower saloon door, clearly shown. (Both: Courtesy Dave Haddock Collection)*

operate 75% of the mileage on these two routes.

A further new service involving not only Grey Green but also Associated Motorways was introduced from Haslingden to Brighton and Eastbourne, operating on Friday nights southwards and Saturday days northwards. Again, this replaced the through-booking system via London or Cheltenham and commenced in 1969.

The same year saw the introduction of a further through-booking arrangement on the Clacton service with Premier Travel. This time to Parkeston, Dovercourt and Harwich by changing onto service 67. Also introduced were 2.15pm Rochdale to Cambridge and 3.00pm Cambridge to Rochdale journeys operating Fridays and Sundays from Spring Bank Holiday to September.

Premier Travel Agency also offered inclusive holidays by service coach, one of which was unusual in that the Clacton - Blackburn service could be extended to the White Bull Hotel in Blackburn to cater for tour passengers.

Introduced in 1972 was a direct Bacup to London service to cover motorway operation south of Manchester. It was the last year of the Bedford to Southport service.

A new service that did not reach expectations was operated jointly with Crosville and Midland Red between Liverpool and Clacton on Sea.

Nineteen-seventy-five saw a major change in the London services with the route between Blackpool and Bolton being withdrawn and replaced by a revised Bacup to London service. Similarly the Haslingden to Rochdale section was withdrawn and replaced by a revised Rochdale to London service. The picking-up points at Blackburn and Accrington had been withdrawn a few years previously. Most of the intermediate fare stages had been transferred to the two Clacton services, including local fares.

New services were also introduced operated jointly with Grey Green and National Travel: Blackpool to Ramsgate, Blackpool to Folkestone, Haslingden to Ramsgate and Colne to Eastbourne. They were operated on a coordinated basis allowing for interchanging at Newcastle under Lyme and replaced the services that dated from the late sixties. There

was also a Colne to Eastbourne service, operated only by National Travel.

A 1976 agreement with National Travel (NBC) involved the transfer of the London services to National Travel (North West), including the feeder services from Todmorden. Yelloway lost its share of operation on the three joint services to Ramsgate, Folkestone and Eastbourne, although Grey Green continued for a short while before coming to an agreement with National Travel, which included other services in the South-East.

As has been shown, Yelloway had perhaps been planning this for some time with the general transfer of destinations from the London services to the Clacton group, which could now be developed further. A typical example the following year was an application, jointly with National Travel (North East) and Premier Travel, for the summer season between Sheffield and Butlins Holiday Camp, Clacton.

This agreement brought about also the resignation from two of his directorships by Hubert Allen. One was of PSV Operators Ltd, who looked after members' interests who operated into London, which now no longer applied. The second was of Travel and Transport, the publishers of *Coaching Journal and Bus Review*, which had been developed from PSV News. The appointment at that company had been as a nominee of PSV Operators Ltd. Herbert Allen had been a Director of both since 1931 and Hubert took over following his father's death in 1956.

Local fares were introduced during the next two years up to Derby and also Blackpool up to Leek and Blackburn up to Stockport. Nineteen-seventy-nine saw the last operation of the Bedford - Morecambe service and the following year found Yelloway facing the traumas of deregulation.

Tours and Excursions

Yelloway operated a full range of day excursions and, prior to 1953, extended tours, which tours included various Scottish Holidays ranging from four to nine days. Although their starting-point was in the North-West, it was possible to join at London using the Yelloway London service with overnight accommodation arranged in Rochdale or Manchester before and

It was not easy to obtain new buses, much less coaches, during the war years. Between 1941 and 1945 Yelloway was allocated only three vehicles by the Ministry of War Transport: two single-deck Leyland Tiger TS11s and a Daimler CWG5 double-decker. The first of the single-deckers, new in March 1942, was **EDK 726**, a Burlingham-bodied - to austerity standards laid down by the Ministry of Supply - 32-seater. In these views it was brand new. (Both: Courtesy David Allen)

after the tours. There were also tours from the North-West to the south coast. All the tours were what was known as Progressive Holidays, where one or more nights were spent in a number of different resorts. In 1953 Wallace Arnold of Leeds purchased the goodwill of the extended tours from Yelloway.

Of the 21 tours licensed to Yelloway, only nine had had their overall charge increased since 1945 to keep up with increased costs. Why the Allens did not increase the inclusive charge including the road fare on all the tours, as other operators were doing, even though they might not be operating the tours at that time, is something researches have failed to elucidate, but it certainly brought problems to Wallace Arnold when they applied to bring the charges up to date. The difficulties can be imagined when it is realised that a nine-day Continental Tour was on offer at an inclusive charge of £10/10s/0d (£10.50) - a remarkable bargain even a half-century ago. Wallace Arnold did try to operate the tours but were not successful and they were gradually withdrawn after an attempt had been made to operate feeder services from the North-West to join Wallace Arnold's own tours from Leeds.

The purchase of William Makinson in 1968 brought some extended tour licences back into the Yelloway fold and attempts were made to operate a small programme.

Yelloway operated an eight-day holiday in Torquay based on the Devonian service with an inclusive charge for coach travel, hotel accommodation and excursions at the resort. It was run in conjunction with Falkland Garages who were also Torquay excursion operators.

Yelloway did not operate, as it had done before 1939, any holidays in conjunction with Associated Motorways to other resorts, although they did participate from the mid 1950s in the Easyway Holidays, originally set up by Ribble and later to include Yelloway and North Western, which covered all the south coast seaside resorts.

In 1947 Yelloway purchased the business of Creams (Lancashire) Ltd from Brierley Brothers of Llandudno. This brought into the Yelloway portfolio a Rochdale - Llandudno service, which was extended to Hebden Bridge and Todmorden during local holiday weeks. Creams had operated an extensive excursions

programme and was operated as a subsidiary with its own coaches.

The next company to be taken over was T H Parker, trading as Blue Bird Motors, in 1956 with their excursion licences being transferred to Creams. Holts of Oldham excursion licences were also taken over and operated as a subsidiary for a short time, though no coaches were owned and were hired in from either Yelloway or Creams. The licences were eventually to be merged with those of the Creams operation.

During 1959 the Rossendale Division Carriage Company Ltd, of Bacup, was taken over, which led to a football service from Stacksteads to Burnley operated jointly with Todmorden Joint Omnibus Committee. As double-deckers were authorised on the licence it is assumed Todmorden took part in the operation.

In the same year Johnston Bros. (Middleton) Ltd and Merriway Tours Ltd of Oldham were acquired, both being merged with Creams.

In 1961 applications were made by Creams and Yelloway to combine their excursion licences into seven jointly held licences. There were two exceptions: the Creams licences in Yorkshire, both express and excursion, remained solely operated by that company while the same applied in Bacup where Yelloway retained the licences. The Traffic Commissioners treated the joint licences as one operator and gave CZ as the licence reference with the former Creams or Yelloway licences being surrendered. For mileage and revenue settlement this was arranged on a 50/50 split between Creams and Yelloway.

1961 also saw the acquisition by Creams of the Turner Brothers (Todmorden) Ltd excursion licences, thus extending their hold on that town. In 1964 the excursion licences of Alice Holt, P R Holt and R D Holt (trading as C Holt and Sons) of Whitworth were merged into the Yelloway/Creams joint licence.

A further purchase was that in 1967 of Kershaws Luxury Tours Ltd. The company was operated as a subsidiary until 1972, with a small number of coaches, after which the licences were merged into the Yelloway operation. The following year, 1968, saw the purchase of the Robert Holt & Co Ltd

Above: This interior view is of **EDK 726**, the Burlingham-bodied Leyland Tiger TS11. *(Courtesy David Allen)*

Below: The other wartime Leyland Tiger TS7, **EDK 740**, is seen as rebodied in early 1947 with an early example of the products of the combine cooperative Trans United. The vehicle was later rebodied again, this time with a fully fronted design. *(John Banks Collection)*

excursion licences from Oldham, these also being merged into the joint Creams and Yelloway operation. This acquisition reforged a link with the Holt Bros. (Rochdale) Ltd company that had failed in 1930, returning to Yelloway a portion of that business that Holt had retained. Holt's company had passed to R Wood & Sons (Tours) Ltd, of Ashton-under-Lyne, and had later been purchased by Eric Stott of Oldham who retained the extended tours part of the business, selling only the day excursions to Yelloway. For completeness, mention is made again of the acquisition of two further companies, which were operated as subsidiaries: William Makinson and North Manchester Coachways.

1970 saw the winding up of the Creams company; their name was deleted from the joint licences and the Yorkshire licences were transferred into the Yelloway name. Licences held by O Smith Ltd, R Jay Ltd, of Littleborough, and J Fletcher were merged into the Yelloway licences although there was agreement with Ellen Smith of Rochdale on these purchases.

In 1973 the licences held by William Makinson were merged into the North Manchester Company and in 1976 that company was wound up with the licences transferred to Yelloway. Lastly the Ribble excursions from Bury were to be operated jointly with Yelloway from 1978, although by the following year the Ribble name had been deleted from the licence.

An additional facility was the operation of period returns to seaside resorts at the various holiday fortnights. These would include Cleveleys, Blackpool, Morecambe, Southport, Aberystwyth, Bridlington, Scarborough and the North Wales coast.

By 1973 there was renewed interest in short-break holidays by the independent operators and various applications were being made. In the eye of the excursion operator the two-day break was a continuation of his day-tour programme and most applied to have these included on their licence. The Traffic Commissioners had from the start of licensing arranged excursion operators into groups so that operators serving the same area charged the same fare. Group 116 served Oldham and surrounding areas. They had had a committee for many years, which represented all the operators and any applications for new excursions were made as a group. This was the case regarding the short breaks in Britain and on the Continent even though many operators did not operate them. There were objections by the established extended tour operators but the Traffic Commissioners granted most licences. So once again Yelloway was involved in the holiday tour market.

Deregulation and competition 1980 - 1984

With deregulation of express services in October 1980 Yelloway would begin to feel "the benefits of competition", to use the politician's fatuous soundbite of the time, on its Torquay route for the first time in nearly 50 years. On 1st November Warner-Fairfax, as part of the British Coachways consortium, began a service between Bristol and Birmingham where connections were available to Glasgow via Altrincham and Manchester. A similar facility was operated by Morris Brothers from South Wales to Birmingham with onward connections northwards.

On 29th April 1981 Warner-Fairfax withdrew from British Coachways and on 16th May a direct service from Paignton to Edinburgh via Birmingham, Manchester and Hamilton was introduced operated by Parks of Hamilton. Route names were also introduced with the new service being called the "Devon-Scot". The service was withdrawn at the end of the summer season and by October 1982 British Coachways had ceased to exist.

There were also other competitors who, during 1981, were to hit Yelloway harder. These were the Friday nights southwards returning Saturday during the day northwards runs operated during the summer months by various coach companies including Shearings of Altrincham, W Robinson of Great Harwood and Smiths of Wigan with Torquay, Bournemouth and Newquay among the destinations offered. They covered a vast number of picking-up points throughout Yorkshire, Lancashire, Cheshire, Greater Manchester and Merseyside. Further services were being offered by operators in the Potteries area, all of which were adversely affecting the Yelloway operation.

Upper and centre: The first new postwar coaches appeared in 1947 and were a batch of four Leyland Tiger PS1s, two with Burlingham and two with Trans United coachwork. One of the latter was **FDK 568**, seen here undergoing its stability test prior to licensing.

Lower: Creams (Lancashire) Ltd was taken over in 1947. The operation was kept on under the Creams name and one of the standard Yelloway vehicles to operate in Creams livery was **FDK 567**, a 1947 Burlingham-bodied Leyland PS1. (All: John Banks Collection)

At the same time National Travel was cutting fares to meet competition from British Coachways as well as other operators that had commenced services over the NT network. This did not help Yelloway: with National's increased services it was now cheaper and sometimes quicker to travel to Bournemouth and Southsea via London than via Cheltenham. Birmingham was also now being developed as an interchange with increased services.

Yelloway reduced the fare to Torquay from £21 return to £18 and also achieved a faster timing by cutting out the Wolverhampton and Kidderminster stops, but were powerless on the connecting services.

National Travel was reluctant to reduce fares where there was no competition, but agreed to a through fare to Bournemouth, Southampton and Portsmouth only from the North-West that was equivalent, if not lower, than the fare via London or Birmingham. These were marketed as "Thrifty" fares and they were not available to passengers starting their journeys in the South. A through ticket was issued instead of two linking at Cheltenham and the scheme began on 7th June.

National Travel also withdrew its early Saturday morning service from Exeter to Cornwall and, as Newquay was a firm favourite for holidays, Yelloway introduced a direct Friday night service to the resort, which also challenged rival operators on the same route. Local fares were introduced between Rochdale and points to Stafford, also from Cheltenham and points up to Torquay thus enabling the company to register part of the service as stage carriage.

National Travel reminded travel agents to the effect that a long-standing agreement existed between National Express and Yelloway Motor Services that passengers had to be booked between a defined area in North-West England or the Potteries and another defined area in South-West England or South Wales. Staff or agents of National Travel were at no time allowed to book or promote bookings for journeys between the areas otherwise than by a Yelloway service.

"Citator", a travel agent who wrote every month in the *Coaching Journal*, took National to task on the legality of this statement and any effort to enforce this regulation by National

could, in his opinion, be referred to the Office of Fair Trading. He ended by saying: "Surely the best way to get more bottoms on Yelloway coach seats was to make sure their services are cheaper, more comfortable and more efficient and not by silly announcements such as I have described above". This sort of nonsense was, presumably, one of the "benefits of competition".

Hubert Allen put it with a subtly different slant in a memo dated 27th June 1981, in which he explained to all his staff the problems they faced and ended by saying: "I therefore call upon all Road Personnel to assist the company not only in retaining its traffic on these services, but also endeavouring to increase the volume of traffic carried. The company has done its part by reducing fares and we would hope that Road Personnel will do their part, and to help us in ensuring that intending passengers and those who have committed themselves to travel believe that it is BETTER TO TRAVEL YELLOWAY and that they will receive better and more courteous attention from Yelloway personnel than if they were to travel by the alternative facilities which have become available". He could have put it a good deal more simply by saying that Yelloway was losing business and everything possible had to be done by all to stem those losses.

From 31st October 1981 the winter service, which had operated to Cheltenham only, was extended to Exeter daily with a further extension to Paignton on Thursday, Friday and Saturday, returning northwards on Friday, Saturday and Sunday. The "Thrifty" fares continued throughout the winter with Stafford being the last picking up point.

National Express operated a service 730 between Birmingham and Plymouth and arrangements were made whereby one timing would be extended to and from Manchester, Oldham and Rochdale. This was operated by Yelloway and began on 7th November. This was to be the first time a Yelloway vehicle had been seen in Birmingham on a regular service since 1930 when a London route was operated for a short while via that city.

Other changes made during 1981 were the introduction of a Rochdale to Ipswich service jointly with Premier Travel. This was numbered 70 and covered points not used

Above: The prewar Bedford WTB had been replaced by the OB in the late prewar period and this model was to become extremely popular in the early postwar years, many lasting in service into the 1960s. **FDK 571** *was one of four with Duple 27-seat coachwork bought by Yelloway in 1947, which lasted only until 1950.*

Below: The postwar Yelloway allegiance to AEC began in June 1947 with three AEC 662 models, GDK 726-8. The middle one of the three, **GDK 727,** *was photographed at Blackpool. Coachwork was by Trans United. (Both: Courtesy Dave Haddock Collection)*

previously, including Altrincham, Hanley and Stafford, before joining the main route at Northampton. The Liverpool to Clacton on Sea service, which had commenced in 1974 with Yelloway as one of the joint operators, was withdrawn.

The 1982 season saw the continuation of services operated in 1981 plus, commencing on 19th June in conjunction with National Travel, service X41 from Rochdale to Bournemouth operating daily via Manchester, Hanley, Coventry, Oxford and Southampton. Special cheap fares were introduced on services departing Friday nights, returning Saturday, to Torquay, Bournemouth, Southampton, Portsmouth and Newquay. The opposition was undercut by up to £3 per head on other services. This kind of manoeuvre, clearly deemed necessary by an experienced and enlightened management striving to cope with "the benefits of competition", could only - with hindsight certainly, but surely it was obvious at the time? - set the company on the slippery slope to oblivion. A further service to Plymouth was introduced on 28th May from Rochdale by-passing Cheltenham and it provided connections to Bristol at Portsmouth. This was in addition to the 730 service jointly operated with National.

Although passengers going on holiday during the summer season were benefiting from the lower fares, the travel agents were not. The number of bookings they were taking did not increase enough to cover the combination of the shortfall in revenue and the decrease in commission received. It was at this period that many travel agents gave up their coach agencies as - as one of them succinctly put it - just not being worth it. It was not until eight years later, when coach operation had settled down and better incentives were given by National Express, that travel agents were again able to realistically consider taking general coach bookings.

The year 1983 saw further new services being introduced, including from 23rd May one direct to South Wales from Manchester via Hanley, Shrewsbury, Hereford, Newport and Cardiff to Swansea where connections were available westward as far as Haverfordwest. Further connections were also available from North Wales via Shrewsbury to South Wales.

These did not last very long: the main route was changed on 18th September to twice-daily via Hanley direct to Newport, Cardiff and Swansea with one timing being extended from Manchester to Oldham and Rochdale. It was the first route to have a National number, 845, while at the same time the X41 Bournemouth service was renumbered 841. Alterations were also made to the Blackpool services, making routes more direct.

On 22nd January 1984 came major modifications when the interchange at Cheltenham, which Yelloway had used since 1936, ceased, although some services still used the coach station. One was the 841 Rochdale to Bournemouth, which had been changed to run via Worcester, Cheltenham and Swindon after leaving Hanley. Interchanging was now done at Bristol with the exception of services to Cornwall, for which transfer was at Plymouth.

Two additional services were introduced: the 885 Rochdale to Bournemouth via Bury, Bolton, Hanley and Bristol, and the 886 Rochdale to Bristol via Oldham and Hanley, which meant that there was a regular two-hourly service between Manchester and Bristol from 8.25am to 2.25pm then 5.25pm.

All Yelloway services were now numbered in the National Express series. The 730 via Birmingham was withdrawn, and just to make life more complicated, a Rapide 547 operated by National Express only was introduced from Bristol to Manchester with special reservations required, which also had special fares.

When the summer timetable was introduced on 20th May the pattern continued as before but connections at Bristol for South Wales were shown for the first time.

The only alteration to the Clacton on Sea services in 1984 was the withdrawal of the Ipswich service to be replaced by an extra Rochdale to Cambridge timing but running via the normal route of Macclesfield and Derby. The route numbers were also brought into the National Express series.

The End 1985 - 1988

By 1985 Hubert Allen was considering retirement. He had been with the company for 58 years. Yelloway was sold on 5th July of that year to A T Lavin, of Carlton PSV. At the same

Above: Trans United coachwork was also specified for 1948 Leyland Tiger PS1 **GDK 303**, seen at Derby bus station in August 1952. (G H F Atkins/© John Banks Collection)

Below: Similar bodywork from Trans United was carried by **HDK 14**, a Leyland Tiger PS2/3, new in September 1949. It was photographed in Anchor Road, Bristol, during a refreshment break on the way to Torquay. (Courtesy Dave Haddock Collection)

time, Trathens of Plymouth, which had ceased trading, was also purchased by Lavin, who also owned a coach firm in Yorkshire called Excelsior. He then formed ATL Holdings Ltd to control all these concerns. Carlton PSV were coach dealers who held the Neoplan franchise and as new owners very quickly disposed of a number of Leyland coaches, including twelve Tigers owned by Yelloway, and in replacement brought in several Neoplan Skyliner double-deckers, which were not looked upon favourably by the older Yelloway passengers who were reluctant to climb - had, indeed, physical difficulties in climbing - the awkward stairs to the upper deck.

Introduced on 27th October 1985 was the Yelloway Rapide consisting of four services daily between Manchester and Bristol with some journeys being extended to various points in the South West.

By May 1986 the company had twelve Skyliners in service with two new vehicles being delivered in National Express Rapide livery. Older AEC Reliances and some Leyland Leopards were retained for services to North Wales, Blackpool and East Anglia.

On 1st June 1986 the company commenced, under Section 34 of the 1981 Public Services Vehicle Act, a service between Bolton and Leeds operating hourly via Bury, Rochdale and Huddersfield.

All the express services, except Blackpool, were now being marketed by National Express and carried its route numbers. The new owners wished to enter stage-carriage operation and applied to operate on services put out for tender by the Greater Manchester PTE. To operate the services granted it was necessary to bring in a fleet of second-hand vehicles.

There were quite a few night services included in the tenders and this meant that vehicles could be operating for 20 hours out of 24. On the first day of stage-carriage operations on "D-Day" 26th October 1986, five of the twelve second-hand acquisitions broke down.

On 27th January 1987 the Bolton to Leeds service was withdrawn and in the same month the Bloomfield Road coach station in Blackpool was closed and the site sold. Vehicles temporarily picked up in the street outside the site until a move into the Coliseum bus station on 16th April. Coaches were garaged overnight at the Squires Gate depot of Fylde Borough Services.

Department of Transport vehicle examiners visited Yelloway's Weir Street premises and found it necessary to issue prohibition and defect notices on the majority of the 42 vehicles examined, which resulted in 81% receiving immediate prohibitions. Vehicles had to be hired in to cover commitments.

On 13th May 1987 the company appeared before the Acting North Western Traffic Commissioner, Keith Waterhouse, to account for the number of notices served on them. In anticipation of the hearing the company had already given notice they wished to reduce the number of vehicles authorised from 60 to 50. On the day of the hearing the Chairman reduced the licence further to 35 vehicles and the company was banned from commencing any more services before their next renewal application in February 1988.

Yelloway appealed to the Transport Tribunal for a stay of the Traffic Commissioner's decision to restrict their operator's licence but were unsuccessful. However, by November the Traffic Commissioners had relaxed the condition and although the company was limited to 29 service licences, new licences could be sought provided that others were surrendered in their place. Recent innovations, such as the Halifax to Blackpool service combining two licences and the surrender of licences for services having expired, allowed the company to apply for new contracts.

On 31st October 1987 Yelloway withdrew completely from the operation of express services with the exception of the Blackpool route. This included the joint operation with Premier Travel on services to East Anglia. All the services involved were reorganised by National Express with ATL Holdings operating certain services on behalf of National Express from their various depots. On 2nd November service 556 Halifax - Ripponden - Oldham, which was operated on behalf of the West Yorkshire PTE, was extended to operate through to Manchester on weekdays. This revived the X12 route commenced by North Western Road Car and Yorkshire Woollen District in 1929. The Blackpool service was operated over the Christmas period but the

Above: By the time 1950's AEC Regal single-deckers were ordered, the model had moved on to the 9621E, otherwise and more familiarly known as the Regal III. A batch of three with Trans United 33-seat coachwork, delivered in March 1950, is represented by **HDK 272**, seen in Derby on its way to London in August 1956.

Below: Yelloway did not at first put all its eggs in one basket, to use the comfortable expression of the era, and orders for Leylands produced Tiger PS2/1s and PS2/3s in 1950 alongside the AEC Regal IIIs. **HDK 420**, a PS2/3 and similarly a Trans United 33-seater, was also in Derby, but in October 1951 and heading for Rochdale. (Both: G H F Atkins/© John Banks Collection)

Rochdale to Blackpool section was withdrawn after operations on 3rd January 1988.

Following further maintenance problems Yelloway again appeared before the North Western Traffic Commissioner but this time for the renewal of their licence. The newly appointed Chairman, Martin Albu, was prepared to give the company one more chance to demonstrate it could put its house in order. He renewed the licence but only for 30 vehicles and reduced the number of local services they could operate to 18. The renewal was for twelve months only.

During the hearing it transpired that all coach work including diagrams for National Express had been moved from Rochdale to either Sheffield or Plymouth and they would not return; in addition there had been another change in management to try and solve the problems. It was further stated that Yelloway had not been profitable since the takeover but with a leaner operation this should be changed. Plans were being made to close Weir Street and find new premises.

With the withdrawal of Yelloway from express services many operators tried to cover certain routes. In 1988 Rothwells of Heywood commenced a service to Blackpool on 31st March while Coachline of Kirkham commenced a further route to Blackpool on 27th May. Rothwells also operated to Torquay and Newquay from Rochdale weekly between 17th June and 15th July to cover local holidays. Ellen Smith and Tatlocks continued to operate to Morecambe and Llandudno respectively, services that had been jointly operated with Yelloway. Abbott's of Blackpool extended their Fleetwood service from Manchester to Hollinwood and Oldham from 2nd May. W Robinson continued with the Torquay, Bournemouth and Newquay services that they had commenced in 1981.

One of the problems with subsidised services was the method of operation. By way of example, in 1988 Yelloway put in tenders for three different services and they obtained all of them. In each case they had offered the lowest rate, but were they profitable rates? The differences were amazing: on the 482-485 Bury to Edenfield routes there were two tenders, one for £65,854 and Yelloway's for £48,100. The Lane Head 439 route had three tenders ranging

from Yelloway's £1,980 to £18,975. All tenders are invited on the basis of Minimum Subsidy Agreements whereby the tenderer retains the revenue derived from the operation of the services and the Executive pays the balance of the cost of providing the service.

Although 42 days' notice had to be given by an operator to cease operation of a service or to commence a new one, it was Greater Manchester PTE policy to try and obtain a replacement company before the withdrawn service finished. Hence a period of seven to ten days was the usual notice given to a company after all the formalities had been completed. GMPTE was also well known for short term contracts and in most cases this meant that extra vehicles had to be obtained to cover the tender. The mechanical condition of these extra vehicles was not always all that it should have been, thus causing extra work for the maintenance staff.

Although the company had hoped to turn the corner with a more controlled operation there were still problems. These came to a head when a Special Meeting of the Transport Committee of the GMPTA terminated all the contracts held by the company from 14th November 1988 and the West Yorkshire PTA made a similar decision and terminated their contracts from 21st November.

On 18th November the Department of Transport Examiners arrived in Rochdale and although only a small number of vehicles was checked most collected defect notices, delayed prohibitions or immediate prohibitions.

Yelloway was closed down by ATL Holdings as from 20th November 1988 and Crosville Motor Services, owned by ATL (Western), in which ATL Holdings Ltd had no financial interest, took over certain contracts for the GMPTE in addition to services from Halifax to Oldham under the West Yorkshire PTE. Apart from seven vehicles transferred from Yelloway to Crosville all other vehicles were passed to Carlton PSV. Other tendered routes in the Greater Manchester area were taken over by Walls, GM Buses, Ribble and Frontrunner (East Midland), and Yorkshire Rider did the same in the West Yorkshire area.

The Chairman of the GMPTA Transport Committee, in a newspaper statement, blamed the Government's Transport Policy for the

Nineteen-fifty-one brought a remarkable sequence of vehicles, consecutively registered HDK 801-6, that included three quite distinct types. The first two, exemplified by **HDK 802**, were Leyland Tiger PS2/1s with Burlingham fully fronted 37-seat bodywork. (Both: John Banks Collection)

downfall of Yelloway, which was undoubtedly true, although he did not mention the problems with the vehicles, which had nothing to do with the Government of the day.

In July 1989 National Express Holdings purchased the ATL Holdings Group, which now consisted of Sheffield Bus operator SUT, Yelloway, Trathens, Excelsior and Carlton PSV. National Express also took control of six travel agencies including the ones originally owned by Yelloway.

Hubert Allen, however, still maintained a stake in the travel industry through a travel agency based in Altrincham run jointly with two former Yelloway managers. On his death at the age of 82 on 24th November 1994 the agency closed and the link forged all those years ago was finally severed.

The demise of Yelloway aroused interest in the trade papers, one of which printed an article entitled "How Yelloway lost its way". Part of it was based on an interview with the new ATL Managing Director who claimed that the company had been "losing money" for four years prior to take over and not only had investment been reduced but the assets that were acquired were then in poor condition. One wonders why the operation was purchased if all that were true. Certainly there were protests from many leading figures in the coaching world who supported the reputation of Yelloway prior to the change of ownership. There was even a letter from the original Yelloway accountants, at the request of Hubert Allen, who was still a non-executive director of ATL Holdings, to put the record straight. Published under the heading "Correct accounts" by the paper it confirmed that for the year ending 31st December 1981 there had been a pre-tax loss of £37,855, but that there had been pre-tax profits in 1982 of £192,862 and in 1983 of £128,184, and that the company had suffered a loss of £107,000 in 1984: those figures add up to a pre-tax profit for the four years of £176,191. With regard to investment in new vehicles, £849,231, paid out of Yelloway's cash reserves, had been spent during the same four years and the accountants concluded that Yelloway always pursued a policy of replacing its fleet on an annual rotating basis and of maintaining its fleet to a high standard of repair and appearance. The latter point perhaps

needed making as part of the refutation, but was, and is, self-evident to anybody who knew the fleet before 1985.

In analysing these figures it should be recalled that in any event 1981 was a difficult year for express operators, faced as they were with the introduction of deregulation and many extra miles were operated in order to lose money as one of the "benefits" of competition; and that in 1984 the introduction of Bristol as the interchange point and consequent new services again involved additional mileage before the public got used to the new network. Therefore, modest losses in those two years were not surprising; were, indeed, perhaps expected as operators strove to survive the chaos of deregulation.

Overall, it is difficult to see how a four-year period showing a pre-tax profit of £176,191, a period that also saw expenditure from reserves of not far short of one million pounds on new vehicles, could be described as "losing money for four years", or as having "assets in poor condition".

It is easy with hindsight to pass comments on the downfall of Yelloway, but could it be opined that a *sine qua non* of good management, especially those considering buying companies, might be the possession, as well as hindsight, of foresight? The author for one, in his old age (this is Keith Healey writing), remembers with fond affection the Yelloway services in the 1950s and 1960s not only as a booking agent but as a traveller. Recording the history of that eminently successful operation, so quickly lost after the Allen guiding hand was removed, is a tribute to fine father and son teamwork, in addition to which must not be forgotten the contribution of all the Yelloway staff who loved their company and responded fittingly to the leadership of Herbert and Hubert Allen.

An appendix of explanatory odds and ends

Duplication

When and how many vehicles could be operated on certain services was governed by the road service licence granted by the Traffic Commissioners. Yelloway had no duplicate restrictions on its main route to Torquay during

*Above: **HDK 803** was the first Yelloway underfloor-engined chassis. It was an AEC Regal IV, which was fitted with distinctive Trans United 39-seat centre-entrance coachwork. (Courtesy Dave Haddock Collection)*

*Below: HDK 804-6 were also underfloor-engined, but on the rival Leyland Royal Tiger chassis, with identical coachwork. The last of the three, **HDK 806**, features in another Derby bus station view. (G H F Atkins/© John Banks Collection)*

the summer months, although there were restrictions on the winter service. Similarly, the Blackpool main route was free of restrictions. However, in the case of the Clacton on Sea and London services they were severely restricted.

Duplication on express services was firstly based on a daily allocation, in many cases, the same on each day. Therefore, weekends became full whilst there were spare vehicles during the week. To overcome the problem, operators from the North-West to London in the 1960s applied for a monthly aggregate with the condition that only a certain percentage of the total, usually 10%, should be used on any one day. This did help Yelloway but they were left far behind in vehicle allowance. As an example, for the month of August in 1963 on the London service to Blackpool they were allowed 142 vehicle journeys whilst Standerwick/Scout on the same route were allowed 2,263 and North Western/Midland Red from Manchester had 837. There were various other restrictions imposed on Yelloway departures, for example between Loughborough and London to protect the United Counties service from Nottingham, as well as the number of vehicles that could be operated between Manchester and London.

On excursions and tours the restriction was on the total number of vehicles allowed each day. By careful scheduling the same vehicle could do a morning, afternoon and evening excursion, thus counting as one vehicle against the allowance for that day.

It was not until October 1980 with the introduction of deregulation for express services that the duplication restriction was removed and services could be operated to meet public demand. There had always been the questions over the years as to whether the restriction helped, was there a need for the railways, or even other road operators, to have artificial protection against operators of road services.

LASCO (Lancashire Air and Seaports Coach Operators)

The development of Continental Holidays, especially those involving air travel, as well as

Travel and Holidays Exhibitions at Manchester's Free Trade Hall in the 1950s were usually graced by an attractive Yelloway display set. (Courtesy Dave Haddock Collection)

Yelloway had, in common with other operators of well-subscribed express services, to hire coaches in quantity to cope with demand on its services, especially at peak periods. These Weir Street, Rochdale, scenes of 1950/1 show a variety of AEC Regals from the Hanson fleet working on the Yelloway service to Blackpool. Identifiable among the six Hanson vehicles visible are **AVH 902**, **EVH 84** and **EVH 808**. In the background of the picture below, a North Western Bristol L5G is emerging from the Yelloway coach station. (Both: Courtesy Dave Haddock Collection)

cruises by ship, brought a problem to the established express service operators. Travel agents, in addition to booking holidays, were putting together package holidays in conjunction with tour operators especially during local holidays in their towns.

Newspaper promotions were also offering special tours, particularly in connection with sea cruises from Southampton. How did the passengers reach a departure point that might be 100 miles away? The answer was for the travel agent or newspaper to hire coaches from a local operator and offer free travel to connect with the holiday. The problem was that it was not free in the strict sense of the word as the hire charge had been incorporated in the inclusive charge and use of the word "free" was to overcome the road service licensing conditions.

Yelloway was first involved in 1960 with a service from Blackburn to Southend airport with later an alternative route to East Midlands airport being granted. Picking-up points were as for the normal Clacton on Sea route between Blackburn and Macclesfield and the operation was exclusively for Gaytours and their holidays to the Channel Islands. The vehicle was hired by that company at a fixed rate thus enabling individual fares to be charged. Standerwick and Scout operated similar services from Blackpool. Yelloway also provided a special service from Rochdale via Oldham to Ringway (later Manchester International) airport. This service was operated on behalf of the Rochdale Observer and Oldham Chronicle for holidays arranged by them.

The express operators were looking to find a way around the private-hire problem and approached this in two ways. Firstly, in 1971, was an application by the North Western Road Car Company, W C Standerwick, Ribble Motor Services and Yelloway for excursion and tours licences originating at Fleetwood and Colne with a number of picking-up points serving the principal sea and airports throughout England and Wales, known as LASCO. A further application from Newcastle under Lyme was made but this was not as open as the first two with various restrictions being placed on it as to which tour operators could use the facility. Further licences were also obtained from North Wales and Cumbria in which Yelloway did not

participate. The other arrangement was for the express service operators, giving Yelloway as an example on the service between Rochdale and Southsea, to have a special condition whereby additional timings could be operated to Southampton docks on behalf of tour operators who would hire the vehicle at a set price. In cases where no direct service was licensed a linking arrangement was made with other operators. Associated Motorways services to London linked at that point with East Kent for Dover and Folkestone ports in addition to small airports within the East Kent operating area used by charter airlines, thus enabling through vehicles to be operated.

It was under the LASCO licences that Yelloway commenced the Paris Rapide service on 7th June 1974; travel was by coach from Rochdale to Dover, hovercraft to Boulogne and finally by SNCF train to Paris in a total journey time of 14 hours. Doubts were expressed as to whether use of the LASCO licence was legal to operate a regular service and an application was made for a licence between Rochdale and Dover, which after objections, was granted for the 1976 season. The service was, however, terminated at the end of the 1979 season.

Grants

In 1974 Hubert Allen demonstrated how an operator of purely express services running throughout the year was unable to claim back under the bus grant scheme. In an article published in a trade magazine he refers to two hypothetical operators, Red Line and Blue Line, both of which operated between points approximately 100 miles apart. Blue Line was licensed as an express service because it had no fare of 11p or under, which was the definition of a stage-carriage service, while Red Line was licensed as stage carriage with a small number of fares below 11p. His argument was that Blue Line could not get any relief, whilst Red Line could get fuel rebate as well as bus grants providing more than 50% of the mileage operated was on stage-carriage operation. Although his comparison was with two companies operating similar services, it was clear that he was in fact referring to the joint service operated to Clacton on Sea on which Premier Travel cooperated. Premier could,

*Above: Hebble Motor Services Leyland-bodied Royal Tiger No. **56** (**CCP 226**) has an "On Hire to Yelloway" sticker in its windscreen as it loads at Yelloway's Blackpool coach station. (Courtesy Dave Haddock Collection)*

*Below: A Mills and Seddon, of Bolton, Trans United-bodied underfloor-engined AEC, **NTC 457**, was similarly stickered when photographed in Anchor Road, Bristol, working on the Yelloway service to Torquay. This operator was another member of the Trans United cooperative. (Courtesy Dave Haddock Collection)*

because of their stage carriage routes around Cambridge, obtain grants on new vehicles including coaches as long as a certain mileage was operated on stage services. By these means, Premier Travel could operate vehicles similar to Yelloway's on the joint service with half the cost spread out over the years. This meant Premier Travel could make a larger profit from the service than Yelloway did after all costs had been taken into consideration. Hubert Allen considered that the stage and express licences should be replaced with a scheduled service licence and if financial aid must be given to one section of the industry, then by all means give it, but it should be given in ways which would not be detrimental or harmful to other sections of the industry. He ended by quoting those famous lines from the Terrence Rattigan play "The Winslow Boy" - "Not only should justice be done - it should be seen to be done".

Since 1976 there had been a 15p single fare between Great Yeldham and Bagthorne End, a journey time of ten minutes. On 27th October 1977 the stage carriage fare requirement was increased to 20p and the Clacton route could now be registered as stage carriage and certain grants could be obtained enabling Yelloway to purchase their first grant-aided vehicle for use on the service.

With deregulation on 6th October 1980, a stage-carriage service was redefined as one on which the same passenger was picked up and set down within a 30 mile radius; this was later reduced to 15 miles. This enabled the Blackpool services also to be classified as stage-carriage routes.

Trans United Coachcraft Ltd

Trans United Coachcraft Ltd was run by a consortium of operators, in which the Allens and Yelloway played a significant part, and was formed in the early postwar period to build bodies for members of the consortium. Later, sales were made to non-members.

The first coach body was built at Weir Street, and is thought to have been that on the 1942 Leyland Tiger TS7 (see page 33) recorded as having been rebodied in February 1947. The coachbuilder Lewis & Crabtree had supplied bodies to Yelloway before the war, and Jack

Crabtree is thought to have been involved in the early stages of Trans United. Premises more suitable than the garage at Weir Street were soon found and the operation went on to produce many bodies, which, by 1952, had graduated to model names: the Borderer and the Dalesman for underfloor-engined chassis, and the Pennine and the Cambrian for forward-engined vehicles.

Yelloway's last Trans United bodies seem to have been supplied in 1951; from the following year Burlingham was the main coachwork provider until it passed into Duple control, after which Yelloway's orders went to Harrington; later, Plaxton became the major suppliers to Yelloway right through to the end of the Allen-controlled company.

The fleet

For the purposes of describing and illustrating the vehicles used on the multitude of services described above, the companies R Holt, Holt Brothers, Holt Brothers (Rochdale) Ltd and Yelloway Motor Services, incorporated on 9th April 1932, will be treated as one continuous operator, which, initially, also operated goods vehicles.

As is so often the case, neither detailed records nor photographs of the very early fleet are conspicuous by their profusion. It is known that at least two Foden steamers had been purchased by 1910, and that the first purpose-built passenger vehicle came in 1913; the years before 1920 saw a series of Dennis, Halley and Belsize chassis acquired, all fitted with *char-à-bancs* bodywork.

In the early 1920s the Dennis remained popular, accompanied by small numbers of Vulcan, Karrier and AEC chassis. From 1926 to 1928 at least 24 Reo coaches, bodied variously by Lewis and Crabtree, Santus, and Davidson, were purchased, many to be repossessed by the hire-purchase company and later repurchased by the operator.

As the twenties gave way to the thirties, Gilford and Tilling-Stevens each sold several chassis into the fleet but as the 1930s got under way the Leyland Tiger and the AEC Regal began to make their presence felt and in the second half of the decade were joined by examples of the Leyland Cub and Cheetah, as

Above: More Leyland Royal Tigers, now with Burlingham Seagull centre-entrance 41-seat bodies, arrived in 1953. **KDK 61** is seen when brand new.

Below: **KDK 62** of the same batch was photographed at Yelloway's Blackpool coach station, with various earlier Leylands alongside. (Both: Courtesy Dave Haddock Collection)

well as a number of Duple-bodied 25-seat Bedford WTB coaches and the first modern double-deckers in the shape of three Leyland TD5 Titans. The Titans were bought for the busy Rochdale to Manchester express service; faced in 1944 with the need to raise finance, Yelloway sold this service jointly to the Manchester, Rochdale and Oldham municipalities, each of which acquired one of the Yelloway Titans (see pages25/7).

The years of the Second World War brought problems to Yelloway as they did to most other operators, and the small number of wartime utility vehicles allocated was insufficient. They were augmented by a handful of second-hand single-deckers, and two double-deckers of the AEC Regent ST class were borrowed from London Transport to help with increased loadings on the Rochdale to Manchester express service.

Again in common with other firms, Yelloway found a return to peacetime standards somewhat slower than might have been expected and it was 1947/8 before the first new coaches arrived. These were Leyland PS1 Tigers with coachwork by Trans United or Burlingham and Duple-bodied Bedford OBs. Postwar AEC Regals appeared in 1949, fitted with Trans United coachwork.

In the period 1950 to 1954 AEC Regal IIIs, Leyland PS2 Tigers and Bedford OBs were delivered, as were the first underfloor-engined chassis: Leyland Royal Tigers and AEC Regal IVs. Duple bodied the OBs again and Trans United and Burlingham shared the orders for coachwork for the heavyweights.

The pattern changed in the second half of the 1950s. The heavy, somewhat over-engineered first-generation underfloor-engined chassis gave way to lighter versions: the Tiger Cub from Leyland and AEC's Reliance. Yelloway invested confidently in the Reliance from 1955 and into the sixties, and, taking the place of the Bedford OB as the lightweight choice, the Bedford SB, the VAM with its set-back front axle and the six-wheeled VAL came in some numbers among all the AEC Reliances.

From time to time vehicles from acquired operators' fleets were taken into use by Yelloway, and new vehicles bought by Yelloway were operated under the name and livery of a subsidiary.

Support for the Southall product remained unshakeable into and through the 1970s and the decade saw many examples with Plaxton, Harrington or Duple coachwork join the fleet.

In 1980, fuelled by the announcement of the suppression of the AEC Reliance chassis by Leyland, who by then controlled AEC, Hubert Allen made an equally wholehearted commitment to Leyland chassis, and the first half of the eighties produced a series of Plaxton-bodied Leopards and Tigers.

Throughout the Allen-controlled period there were many coach hirings. In the summer of 1982, for example, vehicles from the O'Donnell of Rossendale, Mostonian of Manchester, Stubbs of Manchester, Leigh of Middleton, Pickup of Rochdale, Healing of Chadderton, Davies of Little Hulton, Jenkins of Skewen and Murray of Blackpool fleets were noted working on hire to Yelloway.

Several genuine Yelloway vehicles have been preserved, including that owned by Dave Haddock, who has been so helpful with material for this book. Dave's vehicle is fitted out as a mobile museum of Yelloway history.

The Lavin era from 1985 brought in a dramatic change, as has been mentioned. The newest coaches - the Leyland Tigers - were quickly sold and there was an influx of Auwaerter Neoplan double-deck coaches and a variety of second-hand single-deck coaches, as well as the second-hand service-bus stock for use in the ill-fated venture into stage-carriage operation.

Vehicles to be seen on the latter included Daimler Fleetlines (many of which had been marketed as "Leyland" Fleetlines when new to London Transport), Bristol VR double- and RE single-deckers, and a variety of Leyland Nationals. Much of this stock was 15 and more years old, was perhaps not as mechanically reliable as it might have been, was not repainted for use by Yelloway and had stickers bearing the "Yelloway" fleetname applied, often carelessly, on top of a kaleidoscope of liveries that bore no relation to anything ever used by the pre-1985 company. It is perhaps not surprising that Hubert Allen in his old age, when talking about these years, betrayed some emotion and confessed that he had tried to avoid going anywhere where he might catch sight of his company's name thus used.

Above: *The Leyland Royal Tiger and the AEC Regal IV were found to be heavier than necessary and were soon replaced by the more lightly engineered Tiger Cub and Reliance. In 1955, Yelloway began a long series of orders for AEC Reliances, beginning in that year with a batch of four with Burlingham 41-seat front-entrance coachwork, of which* **MDK 918** *was in a damp Derby bus station on its way to Blackpool. Behind was Leyland Royal Tiger* **KDK 61**. *(G H F Atkins/© John Banks Collection)*

Below: *Genuine Burlingham bodies were carried by the 1955-9 Yelloway Reliances, but in 1960 the coachbuilder came under the control of Duple. An immediate result was a batch of four AEC Reliances with Duple coachwork in June 1960. This one is* **WDK 952**, *from the batch WDK 950-3. (Courtesy Dave Haddock Collection)*

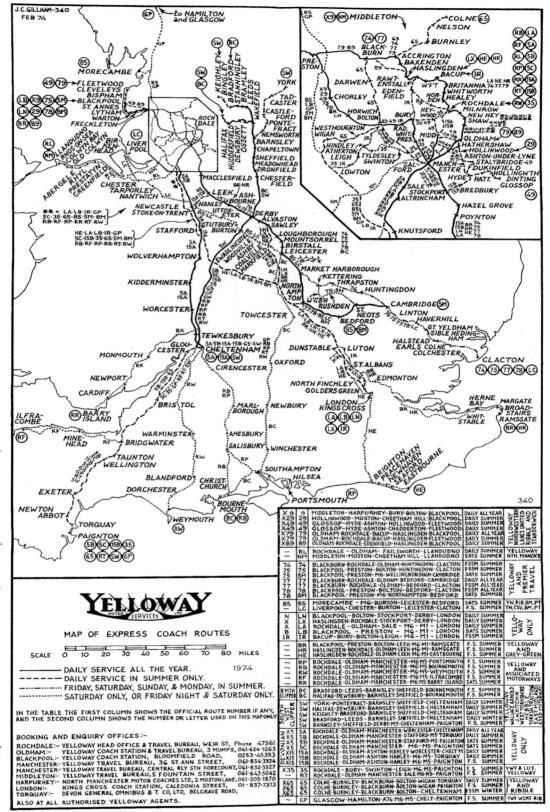

Above: It is possible that the Duple coachwork did not please, for Yelloway soon transferred its orders to Thomas Harrington, of Hove, a batch of six (YDK 585-90) Cavalier-bodied 37-seat AEC Reliances appearing in 1961. **YDK 587**, in another Derby bus station view, provides a direct comparison with the previous year's Duple machines, one of which stands behind. (G H F Atkins/© John Banks Collection)

Below: YDK 585 of the same batch is seen taking part in the 1961 Blackpool coach rally. (Courtesy Dave Haddock Collection)

Above: An unusual chassis to find in Yelloway service was the Ford Thames trader. **YDK 591** was fitted with Duple 41-seat coachwork. (Courtesy Dave Haddock Collection)

Below: Three consecutive seasons' deliveries of AEC Reliances are shown from right to left in this view at King's Cross coach station on 25th August 1962: 1962's Harrington-bodied 45-seater **2927 DK** was the last of a batch of seven in that year; alongside was **YDK 587**, a 1961 Harrington-bodied 37-seater and **WDK 950** of 1960, fitted with Duple coachwork. (Courtesy John C Gillham)

Above: *Since the last Bedford OB in 1950 the Allens had not bothered overmuch with lightweight chassis, but in 1962 started a trend of buying two Bedford SB 41-seaters each season, a trend that persisted to 1966, though in that year the vehicles were Bedford VAM 45-seaters. These Bedfords seem to have worked only one season before being sold.* **2803 DK** *of June 1962, an SB5 with Plaxton coachwork, was the first of them. (Courtesy Dave Haddock Collection)*

Below: *Yelloway's first Bedford six-wheeler, on a VAL14 chassis, came in March 1964. Representing a small batch of two was* **6693 DK** *at Derby bus station later that year. (G H F Atkins/© John Banks Collection)*

Above: Harrington Legionnaire coachwork was tried on Bedford VAL chassis in 1965, as shown on **CDK 410C**, but it bore no resemblance to the stylish Harrington product seen on contemporary AEC Reliances. (Eric Ogden Collection)

Below: The rather odd-looking version of Plaxton's Panorama coachwork that had a distinct variation in appearance for the front bay pillars and some heavily applied brightwork separating that bay's windows from the lower panels, is well shown in this view of Yelloway Bedford VAL14 **HDK 44E**, photographed at Earls Court where the as-yet unregistered vehicle was exhibited at the 1966 Commercial Motor Show. (Courtesy Dave Haddock Collection)

*Above: Bedford VAL **HDK 44E** entered service in 1967. Here it is in April of that year at Derby bus station, on a journey to Clacton on Sea. (G H F Atkins/© John Banks Collection)*

*Below: The same rather garish styling was applied to the 1968 batch of Plaxton-bodied AEC Reliances. There were six, KDK 800-5F, of which **KDK 804F** is shown working the X49 service from Glossop to Fleetwood. (Geoff Coxon)*

Above: The 1970s would see a remarkably stable run of Plaxton-bodied AEC Reliances enter the Yelloway fleet. A typical example was **TDK686J** of May 1971, seen here on the X79 to Oldham from Fleetwood. The coachwork was to a revised, crisper, cleaner styling.

Below: The last new AEC Reliances bought by Hubert Allen were five T-registered examples with the usual Plaxton 49-seat coachwork, WDK 561-5T, delivered in April 1979. Pictured is the last Yelloway Reliance of all, **WDK 565T** (chassis number 38239). This chassis was completed at Southall on 13th November 1979 and was followed by another 97 Reliances before the very last, chassis number 38836 completed on 20th March 1979, bodied by Duple for the dealer Kirkby and eventually going to East Pennine, of Marsden, as FCX 580W, in March 1981. Some of the others entered service as late as 1982. (Both: Geoff Coxon)

Above: Although Hubert Allen could no doubt have had some of those 97 late AEC Reliances, Leyland, by then owners of AEC, was discontinuing the model and operators were being given the hard-sell for the Leyland Leopard (itself shortly to be discontinued). Some were not tempted and bought Volvos but Hubert, a staunch supporter of things British, was convinced by the Lancashire chassis builder's blandishments, buying eight Leopards in 1980/1. The first four, new in July 1980, are represented by brand new **CTD 132V** photographed in that month. (Geoff Coxon)

Below: The second four Leopards, in 1981, were very similar 49-seaters. Geoffrey Atkins found one of them, **MRJ 101W**, at Paignton during his holiday in that resort in June 1982. (G H F Atkins/© John Banks Collection)

Above: Leyland's replacement for the Leopard brought a celebrated model name back into the manufacturer's catalogues. The Tiger was a more sophisticated machine and was immediately popular. Yelloway took a total of twelve in the years 1982-4, all bodied by Plaxton as either 53- or 49-seaters. The first Yelloway Tiger was one of the 53-seaters and was delivered in February 1983. **FWH 37Y** *was photographed at St Margaret's bus station, Leicester, in July 1983, working a timing to Blackburn.*

Below: The 49-seat version had a higher floorline, as shown on **FWH 40Y** *at Paignton bus station in June 1983. (Both: G H F Atkins/© John Banks Collection)*

Above: The last genuine Yelloway coaches were five Leyland Tigers ordered for the 1984 season and bodied, as might have been expected, by Plaxton. They were the first (and only) prefix-registrations for the genuine Yelloway, epitomised by an immaculate **A578 KVU**, a November 1983 delivery.

Below: The Lavin era brought about as exotic a change from earlier standards as could be imagined when it opened with the arrival of two new Auwaerter Neoplan N122/3 77-seat double-deckers, of which we illustrate **B668 DVL** (the other was B672 DVL). Nothing remotely like them had ever borne Yelloway livery and they could, at that early stage of this new chapter of the company's history, perhaps have been seen as a pointer towards a confident and optimistic future that was, alas, not to be. (Both: Geoff Coxon)

*Above: Auwaerter Neoplans also came in the single-deck version, although this example, **FTL 653X**, was second-hand, having been new in 1982 (as EFW 854X) to a Colsterworth operator.*

*Below: Among the new and second-hand Neoplans came an influx of second-hand coaches on a variety of chassis, including two Leyland Leopards with Plaxton 49-seat toilet-fitted coachwork, SPY 372/3X, of which we illustrate **SPY 373X**. These Leylands dated from March 1982 and had been new to the operator Martindale, of Ferryhill, County Durham. The livery treatement was perhaps neither as subtle nor as refined as any of the genuine Yelloway schemes, and with this sign of a falling-off from Allen standards it is meet to draw a veil over the inexorably accelerating decline and imminent demise of a traditional and much-respected institution. (Both: Geoff Coxon)*